THE EYES OF GOD

LIVING DISCERNMENT

BRIAN GALLAGHER MSC

COVENTRY
PRESS

Published in Australia by
Coventry Press
33 Scoresby Road
Bayswater Vic. 3153
Australia

ISBN 9780648566168

Copyright © Brian Gallagher 2019

All rights reserved. Other than for the purposes and subject to the conditions prescribed under the *Copyright Act*, no part of this publication may be reproduced, stored in a retrieval system, or transmitted in any form or by any means, electronic, mechanical, photocopying, recording or otherwise, without the prior permission of the publisher.

Scripture quotations are from the *New Revised Standard Version Bible*, copyright 1989, Division of Christian Education of the National Council of the Churches of Christ in the United States of America. Used by permission. All rights reserved.

Cataloguing-in-Publication entry is available from the National Library of Australia http://catalogue.nla.gov.au/.

Cover design by Ian James - www.jgd.com.au
Text design by Megan Low (Filmshot Graphics FSG)

Printed in Australia

Contents

Foreword   5

Introduction   7

The Way of Freedom   15

    Freedom in Human Experience 16
    Growth in Inner Freedom 24

The Contemplative Way   33

    Prayer...................................... 34
    Contemplation 38
    The Sounds of Silence 46

The Way of Discernment   51

    Conflicting Spirits 52
    God's Spirit in the People of God 63
    God's Spirit in Creation 66

A Way of Life   73

    Living 'in the Spirit' 74
    A Discerning Way of Life.................. 76
    Making Good Decisions 79

Conclusion   91

Afterword   93

Appendix   95

    Awareness Examen 95

Acknowledgments   97

Recommended Reading   99

Foreword

Classical writers in spirituality – Teresa of Avila and John of the Cross, Ignatius Loyola, Hildegard of Bingen, Thomas Merton – wrote from the personal experience of God in their lives. The value of their teachings is that reflection on their own experience led them to deeper insight and new appreciation of the ways of God in other human lives. Much of their personal experience is found to be universal human experience.

In this book, Brian Gallagher writes in the same way. Brian has extensive experience as a spiritual director and supervisor of other spiritual directors, and as a teacher in spirituality, but, more importantly, he has an ability to reflect on and learn from his experience. As a colleague and friend, having ministered with Brian for many years, I have witnessed his profound sensitivity and accuracy in identifying the inner movements prompted by the Spirit of God and those movements prompted by some spirit not of God, both in himself and in those to whom he is ministering. This sensitivity to the ways of the spirits is evident also in Brian's writing. The Spirit is alive in these pages.

I affirm Brian's insistence that living a discerning way of life involves much more than making good decisions. Only when we know the ways that the spirits work in our personal experience will we be free for decision making. This is especially true of our awareness of how spirits not-of-God too easily lead us away from the invitation of God's Spirit. The subtlety of these spirits, tempting at a person's vulnerability, is not widely appreciated. Though we are created free and are called to be free, in practice, our experience of limited freedom exposes us to the promptings of other spirits – and even makes their promptings seem attractive. Brian explains this in detail, writing from his experience.

This is a unique book, blending quite revealing personal experience of God and sound, helpful teaching about the ways of God's Spirit in individual lives and in community. The book will be of value to spiritual directors and pastoral ministers, indeed, to all people who take God seriously and are committed to living a discerning way of life.

Sue Richardson pbvm
Vicar for Religious, Archdiocese of Melbourne
Chaplain, Yarra Theological Union

Introduction

> *The prophet is one*
> *who sees the world with the eyes of God.*
> Abraham Heschel[1]

We live in a world of conflicting attractions and conflicting claims on our choices, indeed conflicting desires. In much of our human experience, it seems as though we want two opposites at the same time. I think of how often I fail to do something that I have committed myself to do. Or I end up following some course of action that I had clearly decided against. Paul captures this experience in that oft-quoted verse that many people seem to identify with:

> I do not understand my own actions. For I do not do what I want, but I do the very thing I hate... I can will what is right, but I cannot do it. For I do not do the good I want... (Romans 7:15, 18, 19)

Examples abound in the literature. Perhaps the best known is from Augustine's *Confessions*. Augustine describes his attraction to both the life of the Spirit and the life of 'the flesh':

---

1 Abraham J Heschel, *The Prophets* (New York: Harper & Row, 1962), 138, 212.

> The two wills within me were in conflict and they tore my soul apart... I was quite sure that it was better for me to give myself up to your love than to surrender to my own lust. But while I wanted to follow the first course and was convinced that it was right, I was still a slave to the pleasures of the second. I had prayed to you for chastity and said 'Give me chastity and continence, but not yet'. For I was afraid that you would answer my prayer at once and cure me too soon of the diseases of lust, which I wanted satisfied, not quelled.[2]

Teresa of Avila knew similar experience:

> I was living an extremely burdensome life, because in prayer I understood more clearly my faults. On the one hand God was calling me; on the other hand I was following the world. All the things of God made me happy, those of the world held me bound. What a terrible mistake, God help me, that in wanting to be good, I withdrew from good...[3]

Teresa admitted that she didn't have the strength to move beyond what she named as some 'attachments' in her heart. These attachments were not bad in themselves, she said, but 'were enough to spoil everything'.

Psychologists explain these experiences in terms of our inner freedom. We are essentially free people, indeed created free, but in practice our freedom is limited – effectively,

---

2 Augustine, *Confessions* (Harmondsworth, UK: Penguin, 1961), VIII, 5-7, 164-9.
3 Teresa of Avila, "The Book of Her Life," in *The Collected Works of St. Teresa of Avila*, ed. Kieran Kavanaugh and Otilio Rodriguez (Washington DC: Institute of Carmelite Studies, 1963), chapters 7, 9, 23.

Introduction

we are not free. What appear to be different tendencies or attractions in our experience are thought to flow from our unconscious places of *unfreedom*. I discuss these in detail in the following chapters.

Alcoholics Anonymous has tackled the experience head-on for people wanting both sobriety and alcohol. Their teaching, the 'Twelve Steps', flowing from their experience, believes that the necessary first step towards freedom is the acknowledgment of one's powerlessness in the struggle and one's need for a 'power greater than ourselves'.[4]

John of the Cross prayed for such inner freedom. His prayer 'make me whole'[5] is a prayer for freedom, at the same time acknowledging the need for a 'power greater than ourselves'. Wholeness is integrity, self-awareness, free choices.

In what follows, I develop essential freedom and effective freedom in human experience and I consider how our inner freedom affects our choices in life. I then discuss how we can become more aware of our *unfreedoms* and how we might grow in inner freedom for the sake of more wholesome, integrated living. Accepting that our freedom is gift of God, I discuss also the place of prayer and openness to that gift.

***

Hindu religions speak of the myth of the white swan. If a white swan is given a mixture of milk and water to drink, the swan will drink the milk and leave the water! The majestic

---

4   Steps 1 & 2 of Alcoholic Anonymous Twelve Step program.
5   John of the Cross, *Centred on Love: The Poems of St John of the Cross* translated by Marjorie Flower OCD (Varroville, NSW: Carmelite Nuns, 1983, reprinted 2002), 22.

white swan becomes the symbol of life's invitation to separate apparent opposites in our inner lives: wheat from weed, good from bad, healthy from unhealthy, the mixed bag of opposing attractions in our human experience. In Sanskrit, the practice of such separation or sifting through inner experience is called 'the science of the water and the milk'[6] and the white swan is the constant reminder of the need for and the possibility of such sifting. The sifting can be as fine as separating milk from water:

> Indeed, the word of God is living and active, sharper than any two-edged sword, piercing until it divides soul from spirit, joints from marrow. It is able to judge the thoughts and intentions of the heart. (Hebrews 4:12)

The importance and the value of sifting our inner experience is that we are then able to decide more freely which of the mixed attractions to follow, indeed which is more life-giving. In the Christian tradition, this is discernment. Discernment is precisely the ability and the habit of sifting through the mixed attractions in our inner lives to discover which lead to healthy life-giving relationships, and which lead away from life. Discernment challenges us to review our inner experience carefully – to see with the eyes of God for the sake of such fine sifting. I discuss below how such fine sifting of our experience becomes more possible with growth in inner freedom.

Much of my ministry, my teaching and my writing focuses on this invitation to sift through our inner experience, to

---

6   Carlos G. Valles, *The Art of Choosing* (New York: Doubleday, 1989), 99.

Introduction

separate opposing attractions. I look back over past writing, much of it unpublished, and I find two recurring themes. I speak often of a way of prayer and living that I call 'contemplative' – not in any remote monastic sense, but in the everyday sense of openness to new awareness – and in numerous places, I bring this contemplative way to my discerning habit of sifting my inner experience.

I recognise now that, though it was not always intentional and not always explicit, my goal has been the integration of these two themes. What emerges is the contemplative spirituality that I consider foundational to living a wholesome way of life. Inspired by the white swan, this book is an attempt to describe that integration.

In my terminology, the tendency or attraction in us that invites to new life, new energy, new loving relationships, I call the Spirit of God, sometimes simply the good Spirit or the Spirit of truth. Whereas any tendencies in us that lead us away from life-giving relationships I call spirits not-of-God, as in a spirit of fear or a spirit of division. Whatever the terminology, the reference is to the inner movements – the attractions and repulsions, the spontaneous impulses and emotions – in our everyday experience.

Noticing these inner movements in oneself calls for a habit of reflection, listening and noticing the movements, then coming to understand from experience the direction in which they lead us. The fruits that emerge when our different attractions are followed are the best indicators of which attraction is more life-giving for us. The Appendix outlines the contemplative prayer called the Awareness Examen, a highly recommended help to this habit of reflection.

I emphasise that this habit of sifting our inner experience precedes any subsequent decision making. My approach focuses on relationships in our life, including relationship with God. I believe that in living our relationships, we are more likely to notice the very personal indicators of the invitation to healthy, wholesome life in our inner experience – and the indicators of any counter attractions. Familiarity with these personal indicators is the best preparation for our life's choices.

I base my understanding and my approach on personal experience, on human values and on values embedded in the Sacred Scriptures. I believe that all spirituality begins with and flows from personal experience. For that reason, the integration of my two themes is both personal and universal: I learn from my personal experience and I develop a broader perspective around wholesome living and making fruitful choices after reflection on that experience.

Introduction

The Eyes of God

The prophet is the one who sees the world with the eyes of God.

Discernment is precisely the habit of sifting through the mixed attractions in our inner lives to discover which lead to healthy life-giving relationships, and which lead away from life.

The fruits that emerge when our different attractions are followed are the best indicators of which attraction is more life-giving for us.

The Way of Freedom

God said: let us make humankind in our image, according to our likeness.
Genesis 1:26

Authentic freedom is an exceptional sign of the divine image in all people.
Vatican II, *Gaudium et Spes* #17

Where the Spirit of the Lord is, there is freedom.
2 Corinthians 3:17

Freedom in Human Experience

Foundational to my faith is the conviction that 'God's love has been poured into our hearts through the Holy Spirit that has been given to us' (Romans 5:5). I find myself constantly listening to and reflecting on what I believe is God's revelation. I believe that God reveals Godself to us – through people, events, my ministry, indeed through my whole life with its many varied and busy involvements.

When I read Cistercian monk Thomas Merton's writing:

> A contemplative is not one who takes his/her prayer seriously but one who takes God seriously...
> one who is famished for truth,
> who seeks to live in generous simplicity, in the spirit.[7]

I understand that to 'take God seriously' means first and foremost to bow before God and to focus on God's presence, God's activity in my life. Life becomes an attitude of openness to God, of listening to and waiting on God in my everyday. The 'Sacrament of the Present Moment' suggests that every moment of every day has the potential to meet God; every person we meet every day becomes a meeting with God. For God is there in every moment, in every experience of every day. To live a spirituality that flows from 'taking God seriously', being 'famished for truth' and 'living in generous simplicity' invites deep inner freedom for the sake of healthy, selfless relationships.

---

7 Thomas Merton, *Spiritual Direction and Meditation* (Collegeville, MN: Liturgical Press, 1960).

God wants us to be *free*. The call to be free is the basic Christian call. And yet, common wisdom is that we all carry some vulnerability; we all have a weak spot in our make-up that limits our freedom. Hence the terminology of *essential* and *effective* freedom'.[8]

Essential Freedom

Christian philosophers, psychologists, anthropologists and theologians all agree that to be human is to be free. Inner freedom is the core of a person's identity.

For example, philosopher Max Muller argues that we can never be deprived of our freedom because it is part of our 'equipment' as human beings.[9]

Psychiatrist and anthropologist, Luigi Rulla, makes the same point:

> The human species is not simply gifted with freedom as other species are gifted, for example, with fins and with wings; I *am* my freedom.[10]

Jesuit Roger Haight, commenting on the anthropology underpinning Ignatius Loyola's *Spiritual Exercises*, summarises:

> ... the primary meaning of freedom equates it with the human person itself: a person *is* freedom.[11]

---

8 Bernard J. Lonergan, *Insight: A Study of Human Understanding* (London: Longmans, Green and Co., 1957), 619-24, 92-3.
9 Max Muller, "Freedom: Philosophical" in *Encyclopedia of Theology: The Concise Sacramentum Mundi*, ed. Karl Rahner (New York: Crossroad, 1975), 535.
10 Luigi Rulla, *Anthropology of the Christian Vocation* (Rome: Gregorian University Press, 1986), 238. Rulla quotes and affirms this comment on the *Pastoral Constitution on the Church in the Modern World* of Vatican II, but does not acknowledge the origin of the comment.
11 Roger Haight, *Christian Spirituality for Seekers* (Maryknoll, NY: Orbis Books, 2012), 87, 103.

A person *is* freedom. To be human is to be free. Even though the human experience of this inner freedom is limited – some say 'flawed' – my experience suggests that one's essential inner freedom is never lost. Indeed, we glimpse our essential freedom from time to time. Even in difficult times, we often sense the possibility of acting quite freely.

Walter who used to visit me regularly for spiritual direction, offers an example of the experience of essential freedom and yet limited freedom.[12]

> **Walter** *began without preliminaries: 'Do you remember my telling you about my friend Wes, the fellow who lost his wife tragically, and then lost his job within a couple of months?' I said that yes, I remember; and I remember that you are trying to support Wes as best you can. 'Well, we went to the races last week; I had a good day and won almost $200 – I gave it to Wes. He pocketed the notes, showed no emotion, and didn't even thank me. I was so caught by surprise that I didn't say anything at the time. But since, I've been quite angry – I'm thinking that I need to confront him in some way. What do you reckon?' My initial response was 'Wal, let's talk first about how this affected you'. Walter was quick to say that he felt taken for granted – 'He obviously doesn't appreciate what I do for him. I don't think I should let him get away with that – that would be too much to ask.' I asked 'How do you mean,*

---

12 This fictitious example is taken from my book *Set me Free* (Bayswater, Vic.: Coventry Press, 2019), 133-4.

> too much – what makes it too much?' 'Well, Wes is $200 better off and I'm left with nothing – no gratitude, no acknowledgment.' 'And that is important to you?' 'Yes' he said with emphasis, and then stopped himself. Slowly, Walter said, 'Do you mean that I could live without being acknowledged and rewarded?' 'Ah, you will have to discover that for yourself, Wal. Would you like to sit quietly with the question, right now?' We did that – for a longer time than I expected – till Walter smiled at me and said 'I really want to stay with this – something's happening – I feel kind-of lighter.' More than happy to wait, I suggested that we talk about it again next time we meet.

Walter would not have imagined that his support for his friend was motivated by anything other than his desire to help someone who was in need. Yet, his feeling 'lighter' seemed to me to be clear sign of a freer place in Walter when he does not act out of his own unconscious need for affirmation. This is not to deny Walter's genuine conscious care for Wes, but to say that at the same time, his helping his friend is motivated also by some degree of self-interest. The possibility of not acting out of that motivation is real and close: Walter glimpses this and responds. In technical terminology, Walter learns self-transcendence.

The Vatican Council document *Gaudium et Spes* teaches that in the exercise of our freedom, we manifest the image of God:

> Authentic freedom is an exceptional sign of the divine image in all people... For God willed that

men and women should be left free to make their own decisions so that they might of their own accord seek their Creator and freely attain their full and blessed perfection...[13]

With this understanding, Rulla and Lonergan both see human freedom as an expression of God's freedom:

... the true and ultimate meaning of man is God himself: God is the only being capable of bringing man to the full realisation of himself.[14]

We are the fruit of God's self-transcendence, the expression and manifestation of God's benevolence and beneficence, God's glory... as the excellence of the son is the glory of his father, so too, the excellence of humankind is the glory of God.[15]

This is the essential freedom, deeply embedded in all people. We are created free, born free.

Effective Freedom

While all people have been gifted with freedom, it is a freedom rarely fully experienced, as suggested in the experiences described in the Introduction.

Freedom becomes something of an ideal, as though removed from our experience and glimpsed only occasionally. The quotation above from the Vatican Council document *Gaudium*

---

13 Vatican II, "Gaudium et Spes (Constitution on the Church in the Modern World)," in *The Documents of Vatican II*, #17.
14 Rulla, *Anthropology of the Christian Vocation*, 148. In this and subsequent quotations, I have not changed the exclusive language of the original writing.
15 Lonergan, *Method in Theology* (New York: Herder & Herder, 1972), 116.

et Spes continues: 'human freedom has been weakened by sin.'[16] Rahner refers to 'the powers of enslavement formed by sin, death and radical selfishness which prevent man from loving God and his neighbour.'[17] These are expressions of the human experience of limited inner freedom. My term *unfreedom* captures this human experience. I stress that this experience is not pathological in any sense. It is normal everyday human experience.

Traditional teaching in spirituality acknowledges the experience of limited freedom, often describing the experience in terms of the self-created image of oneself, the person one thinks one should be. Many of us, unconsciously, imagine that we *have to be* someone or other, or we *have to have* something or other. Such a self is self-created, not God-created. It has no basis in reality, no matter how virtuous it may appear or how much time and energy have gone into cultivating it.[18] Keating calls it 'a homemade self that does not conform to reality.'[19]

Yet, our self-image has a strong influence on our freedom:

> The image we have of ourselves – one component of 'identity' – deeply affects how we meet the world and the attitudes with which we encounter images of God. One's image of oneself is no more real than one's image of God. We are at core endlessly mysterious, and our self-images are

---

16   Vatican II, "Gaudium et Spes (Constitution on the Church in the Modern World)," in *The Documents of Vatican II*, #17.
17   Karl Rahner, *Meditations on Freedom and the Spirit* (London: Burns & Oates, 1977), 37.
18   Thomas Merton, *New Seeds of Contemplation* (New York: New Directions, 1972), 34.
19   Thomas Keating, *The Human Condition* (New York: Paulist, 1999), 14.

simply expedient symbols of who we really are. This is true also for our images of God.[20]

In other words, when we approach God by putting on our 'best' self-image, we encounter only the unreal God of our own imagination. Growth in freedom will mean bringing these false images into awareness in order to transcend them, as discussed below.

The term *attachments* is commonly used to describe those areas of one's inner life that are unfree. For example, some people become attached to their reputation (being well thought-of) or to an ordered life-style (everything always in its proper place) or to their poor self-image (no one cares about me), showing itself in the way they live and relate to other people. Teresa of Avila introduced the term 'attachment', as cited in my Introduction, when reflecting on her struggle to be free in her relationships.

In psychological terminology, 'attachments' are called 'addictions' or inner 'needs'. An addiction is 'a state of compulsion, obsession or preoccupation that enslaves a person's will and desire.'[21] A need is defined as a compulsive tendency to act in a certain way. If a person needs to be well thought of, for example, their behaviour will aim to bring this about. And so, the needs conflict with a person's more conscious values in life.

I emphasise that the experience is of inner attachments. Attachments are experiences of *unfreedom* or limited freedom

---

20 Gerald May, *Care of Mind, Care of Spirit* (San Francisco, CA: Harper & Row, 1982), 66.
21 Gerald May, *Addiction and Grace* (San Francisco, CA: HarperSanFrancisco, 1988), 13-4.

in our inner life. These attachments or *unfreedoms* in our inner life become places of vulnerability where spirits not-of-God are more prone to tempt us. I develop that in what follows. I discuss, first, how we might grow in inner freedom, becoming more aware of and rising above our places of *unfreedom*.

Growth in Inner Freedom

God said 'Ask what I should give you.'
Solomon replied 'give your servant an understanding mind
to govern your people,
able to discern between good and evil.'
God said to him 'I now do according to your word.
Indeed I give you a wise and discerning mind.'

1 Kings 3:5-11

The Scripture tells us that God was pleased that Solomon did not ask for anything *for himself*, like power or riches. God answered Solomon's prayer: 'I give you a wise and discerning mind...' (in another translation, 'a heart wise and shrewd'). The wisdom that God gave to Solomon, it seems, was not a gift *for himself*. Like all of God's gifts, the gift of wise discernment is given for others' sake: it is to be shared. Though given to an individual, many others will reap the fruit. How does this happen?

We all know wise people. I always considered my father a wise old fellow: he was someone I looked up to, someone to whom I would readily go for advice, and someone who gave his advice freely and generously. Indeed, there seems to me to be some essential connection between wisdom and generosity. My parents were extraordinarily generous – with their possessions, their time, their interest and their affection. They may not have articulated it in as many words, but my parents seemed to know that their blessings in life were not solely *for themselves*. And so, they held what was 'theirs' quite lightly; they could just as easily share it with others, even give it away. They took generosity for granted.

This inner freedom – to be able to hold lightly what belongs to us – seems to me to be the link between generosity and wisdom. Both gifts are evident in people who are interiorly free; and clearly both gifts are to be shared. Solomon knew such freedom... and knew it as gift.

In truth, few of us come to *any* relationship utterly freely, whether our relationship with God, with Jesus, with our loved ones, or with people to whom we minister. Invariably, we come with some level of possessiveness or self-interest, though we rarely know this in our awareness. Walter gives a perfect example in the previous chapter. John of the Cross says that the normal development of any relationship is a process of *purification* of our desires, of our love for another. This seems to happen, for example, in a time of crisis in a friendship, a time of frustration in our helping or being helped by another, a time of apparent loss in our lives, or a time when God seems remote and uncaring. At these times, when life seems just too hard, when it seems we just can't pray, when we risk losing heart, and when we find ourselves helpless to change what seems to be happening to us, we are being purified. I develop this process of purification in what follows, stressing the interrelatedness of contemplative prayer, growth in inner freedom and compassionate relationships.

This is the experience John of the Cross calls a '*dark night*.'[22] Though it may be dark and joyless, he says it is the way our desire is purified and freed. It doesn't feel like it, but he says it is a time of grace, a time of inner growth, personally and

---

22 See, for example, Brian Gallagher, *Set me Free* (Bayswater, Vic.: Coventry Press, 2019), 264-76.

relationally. And, John emphasises, it is normal growth – in *life*, as much as in what we might call our spiritual life, and in all our relationships, as much as in our relationship with God.

Gerald May summarises:

> The dark night is a profoundly good thing. It is an ongoing spiritual process in which we are liberated from attachments and compulsions and empowered to live and love more freely. Sometimes this letting go of old ways is painful, occasionally even devastating. But this is not why the night is call 'dark'. The darkness of the nights implies nothing sinister, only that the liberation takes place in hidden ways, beneath our knowledge and understanding. It happens mysteriously, in secret, and beyond our conscious control. For that reason it can be disturbing or even scary, but in the end it always works to our benefit.[23]

Influenced by John of the Cross, Thomas Keating teaches that the practice of centering prayer is the surest way to inner freedom. Stressing that the process of purification is God's work, Keating refers to it as a 'divine therapy'.[24]

The examples from Teresa of Avila and Augustine given above emphasise that such growth in inner freedom depends on God's gift. In Teresa of Avila's example of *unfreedom* – her attachment to some friendship she imagined she couldn't live without – she tells us in her autobiography that she struggled

---

23 Gerald May, The Dark Night of the Soul (San Francisco, CA: HarperSanFrancisco, 2004), 67.
24 Keating, *The Human Condition*, 33.

for twenty years with her ambivalence around wanting to let go, but not wanting to, at the same time. The problem was not the friendships, but her attachment, her *unfreedom*. Teresa describes quite graphically not only how unfree she experienced herself (her word is 'bound'), but also how utterly unable she was to do anything about it.[25] Augustine had the same ambivalent experience when he prayed for years: '*Lord, make me chaste, but not yet!*'[26] In such experiences, we can only wait on God's gift of love.

Some of us, sometimes, may need professional therapy to get to the bottom of some deep-rooted, unconscious *unfreedom*. But most of us, most of the time, find that the give-and-take, the ups-and-downs of everyday life – especially being true in our relationships – give us ample opportunity to grow in freedom. We help ourselves towards inner freedom by honest reflection on our everyday experience, listening to God's Word and God's invitation in our experience. As we wait on the gift, we pray that we may let go of whatever in ourselves we are hanging onto, without realising it.

John of the Cross' poem *Spiritual Canticle*[27] speaks about growth in inner freedom:

> *You looked with love upon me*
> *and deep within, your eyes imprinted grace,*
> *this mercy set me free*
> *held in your love's embrace*
> *to lift my eyes adoring to you face.*

---

25 Teresa of Avila, "The Book of her Life", chapters 7,8,9,23.
26 Augustine, *Confessions* (Harmondsworth, UK: Penguin, 1961), Book 8.
27 John of the Cross, *Centred on Love: The Poems of St John of the Cross*, 20.

Only God's love sets us free. In the experience of God's looking upon us with love, we are set free. Jules Chevalier, founder of the Missionaries of the Sacred Heart, was convinced that God's love, revealed in the Heart of Jesus, is the answer to all the ills in the world. I'm sure Chevalier included all the personal 'ills', the ills inside our hearts, as much as the ills in society. He knew that when we know God's love in our lives, then we are healed and freed.

Teresa says that she hadn't seen 'how little benefit it is if we do not place our trust in God. and lose completely the trust (we have) in ourselves'. Teresa described her final surrender to God in that powerful, simple story when she threw herself at the feet of the statue of the wounded Christ 'with the greatest outpouring of tears' and then: 'I think I said that I would not rise from there until he granted me what I was begging him for.'[28]

Pope Francis often speaks of the gift of God's love. In his encyclical *Laudato Si* – on the care for our common home – he stresses God's love for all people and all creation in sentences like 'God's love is the fundamental moving force in all created things' (#77). The Pope's emphasis on the inter-connectedness of all creation united in God's love, is the foundation of his ecological theology. In recent times, the same emphasis has also encouraged feminist theology, acknowledging the equality of all people, men and women.

This focus on growth in freedom flowing from God's gift of love has numerous implications. For example:

---

28 Teresa of Avila, *Book of her Life* in *The Collected Works of St. Teresa of Avila*, chapter 23.

Focus on right behaviour	Focus on God's gift
Christian life focuses on right behaviour	Christian life is based on the gift of grace
What a person does is primary	*Who a person is* is primary
Emphasis on 'try harder': prayer and holiness are about self-discipline and effort	Emphasis on allowing God to be God, waiting on God's gift of love
Right behaviour earns praise, wrong behaviour earns punishment	Trusting God's call and God's love leads to inner freedom
The risk is a sense of God dominated by fear and judgment	Sense of God imbued with confidence in God's love and mercy

Ignatius Loyola has the same emphasis on growth in inner freedom in his *Spiritual Exercises*.[29] Ignatius' approach focuses on relationship with Jesus, in our desire 'to know you more clearly, love you more dearly, and follow you more nearly'. His recommended prayer exercises are based on his belief that

---

29 Ignatius Loyola, *The Spiritual Exercises of St Ignatius*, ed. Louis J Puhl (Chicago, IL: Loyola University Press, 1951).

our contemplating Jesus in his historical life will challenge us around our unfree attitudes, and so invite us to growth in freedom. In other words, we come to know ourselves more truly as we come to know Jesus.

In this process of purification or growth in freedom, we become more self-aware and more able to sift the mix of movements, the attractions and repulsions in our inner world. As well, we come to know other people as they are, not judged by our likes and dislikes. We are more able to set aside any preconceived ideas about what others expect from us and to allow God to reveal to us how best to respond to the people to whom we are relating. In this process of purification, we move from loving or being with others because of the satisfaction we feel or the affirmation we receive, rather to loving and ministering to others for *their* sake. In our relationships, we are liberated from any self-absorption – we become more compassionate. God's love permeates our lives. Our inner freedom becomes a way of living.

In *Evangelii Gaudium* (#8), Pope Francis says that only when we are set free by this love of God, will our commitment and our mission, our care for other people and our concern for justice bear good fruit:

> *Thanks solely to this encounter with God's love* (the Pope is talking of a person's inner experience), *which blossoms into an enriching friendship, we are liberated from our narrowness and self-absorption... Here we find the source and inspiration of all our efforts at evangelisation.*

At the same time, John of the Cross is quick to point out that purification doesn't happen once and for all: it is an ongoing process, indeed a life-time process of growth in inner freedom. Accepting that the growth flows from God's gift of love, an attitude of openness to the gift is crucial. I discuss now how our prayer practice prepares us for God's gift and how the gift seems to be given in human experience.

The Way of Freedom

The call to be free is the basic Christian call... To be human is to be free.

My term *unfreedom* captures the human experience of limited freedom... This is normal everyday human experience.

The term *attachments* is commonly used to describe those areas of one's inner life that are unfree.

Few of us come to any relationship utterly freely... John of the Cross says that the normal development of a relationship is the purification of our desires, of our love for another.

In the process of purification, we move from loving or being with others because of the satisfaction we feel or the affirmation we receive, rather to loving and ministering to others for *their* sake, regardless of the cost.

Growth in freedom depends on God's gift... Only God's love sets us free.

The Contemplative Way

... we need to recover a contemplative spirit which can help us to realise ever anew that we have been entrusted with a treasure which makes us more human and helps us to lead a new life. There is nothing more precious which we can give to others.

> Pope Francis, *Evangelii Gaudium* #264

Prayer

I believe that being prayerful is more important than saying many prayers. Indeed, Thomas Merton once wrote that 'saying prayers can become an obstacle to prayer.' I think this is because of the risk that overly focusing on how we are praying can distract from a focus on God, the one to whom are praying. Karl Rahner teaches:

> Our love of God and our prayer have one difficulty in common: they will succeed only if we lose the very thought of what we are doing in the thought of him for whom we are doing it... We succeed in prayer and in love only when we lose ourselves in both, and are no longer aware of how we are praying or in what manner we are loving.[30]

I suspect Pope Francis had this in mind when he said that we are to be 'poets of prayer'. Whatever did the Pope mean by 'poets of prayer'? I offer these suggestions.

Once, inspired by a statue of Teresa of Avila called *Teresa in Ecstasy*, I wrote:

> *Ecstasy*
> *Wide open mouth*
> *Wide wide opened heart*

That isn't strictly a poem, I know. Nor is it strictly a prayer. Its only claim to any fame is that the words seemed inspired when I wrote them. I didn't set out to write the words, I didn't

---

30 Karl Rahner, *On Prayer* (New York: Paulist Press, 1968), 31.

think about what I was writing. They seemed to be given to me. It happened one other time: I woke from a dream with these words on my lips:

> *I will see*
> *the face of God*
> *in her loveliness*

Again it seemed as though the words were inspired, given to me. It was as if someone else was writing. I suspect that that is the way of good poetry and good prayer: it is inspired.

The Scriptures encourage 'let the Spirit pray in you'. My experience is that in time we do gradually become more able and willing to let the Spirit pray in us, to let God take over. I think that gradually we become more receptive, more open to God and to other people. I don't mean that we neglect our own experience and our own wisdom, but it seems we become freer about it. We seem able to hold our opinions more lightly, without having to insist on our own way. That makes a big difference to the way we pray.

If we are to let the Spirit do the work, to pray in us, then we don't have to work so hard ourselves, we don't have to try hard to pray. We can wait on God's Spirit. Whether we are working or sitting quietly or taking our daily walk, we do just that. We work, we sit, we walk, we are present to where we are and what we are doing – and we wait on God's inspiration. It seems that all we need to do is to slow down and to be present to where we are and what we are doing – the practice called 'mindfulness'.

This slowing down needs to be in our inner life, not only in the external, more physical activities. We need to slow down our mind and we need to slow down our expectations on what should be happening in our lives.

Slowing down is helped by focusing on our breathing, being present is helped by having just one focus, a mantra word or a visual object. I notice how people who visit my place often sit for ages simply looking at the view. The rhythm of the waves is enough to hold their attention and hold them in the present moment. It seems to me that the normal development of prayer for most people is that our prayer becomes less active, quieter, simpler, more open to God's Spirit praying in us.

A few years ago, I had the opportunity to live in a Zen centre for some months. Curiously, it was the practice of Zen (which the teacher defined simply as *contemplation*) that helped me bring together my own experience of prayer and my years of study in spirituality. In Zen, there's a story about two little fish swimming around in a fish-bowl. The younger fish says to the other: 'what's water?' That's the whole story: no explanations, no applications to one's life: the story says it all.

Zen helped me not only with concentration, focus and stillness, but also with perspective on life. Perspective on God, too. Zen helped me to still my active mind and to let go of thinking about God, 'solving' God. Like the fish, I gradually learned *to be* in God. Such prayer doesn't need thinking; it doesn't seem to need many words; and, in my experience, it doesn't contain much emotion. It is about being present -- even when the presence is far from felt. It is about waiting on God's gift.

The Contemplative Way

Thomas Merton described his way of prayer:

> I have a very simple way of prayer.
> It is centered entirely on the presence of God and
>   on his will and his love.
> That is to say, it is centered on *faith*,
> by which alone we can know the presence of God...
> It does not mean imagining anything or conceiving
>   a precise image of God,
> for to my mind this would be a kind of idolatry...
> There is in my heart this great thirst to recognise
>   totally
> the nothingness of all that is not God.
> My prayer is then a kind of praise
> rising up out of the centre of nothingness and
>   silence...
> It is a direct seeking of the face of the invisible.
> Which cannot be found unless we become lost in
>   him who is invisible.[31]

Merton says what I would like to have said about my own prayer!

---

31 Thomas Merton: a private letter to Abdul Aziz, quoted in William H. Shannon, Christine M. Bocken, Patrick F. O'Connell, eds, *The Thomas Merton Encyclopedia* (Maryknoll NY: Orbis, 2002), 458.

Contemplation

In his classic work on the prophets, Abraham Heschel called the prophet the person 'who sees the world with the eyes of God'.[32] The prophet is not interested in prophesising, looking to the future. Rather the prophet looks to the present reality, wanting to see the world, see other people, and see oneself truly. The prophet wants to see as God sees, 'with the eyes of God'. The prophet would be the true contemplative, the one who looks and waits on God's revealing the truth of life.

In *The Living Flame of Love,* John of the Cross wrote that 'contemplation is to receive'.[33] This has prompted many to see Mary, the Mother of Jesus, as the prototype of the contemplative person. Mary received the Word of God literally in her womb and symbolically in every facet of her being. Mary is sometimes called the 'Womb of God'. The womb is symbol of complete openness and receptivity, of expectant waiting, of total surrender, and of course, of giving flesh and birth to God's Word. The womb is pure receptivity, waiting to receive what will begin the life-process within it. Such openness and receptivity defines the contemplative way that every Christian is called to, all of us receiving and giving birth to God's Word. It is the way to inner freedom.

Human people are by nature contemplative beings, even though the human tendency towards independence and self-sufficiency can be a strong obstacle to 'receiving' for many

---
32   Heschel, *The Prophets* (New York: Harper & Row, 1962), 39.
33   John of the Cross, "The Living Flame of Love," in *The Collected Works of St. John of the Cross*, stanza 3.36.

people. The contemplative approach is helped by an intentional focus outside of ourselves. Whether the object of contemplation is a beautiful flower or another person or the Word of God in prayer, the focus is entirely on the other, with no expectations or pre-conceived ideas about whatever the other will reveal of itself. In the contemplative way, we wait on whatever will be revealed. We wait on God's inspiration. And we remain open to that revelation.

Isaac Newton brought a contemplative stance to his scientific work:

> I keep the subject constantly before me and wait till the first dawnings open slowly, by little and little, into a full and clear light... Truth is the offspring of silence and meditation.[34]

Doubtless, many research scientists do exactly the same, as they wait on and work towards the truth contained in the mystery they are studying, but which is yet to be revealed. Similarly, many spiritual directors and counsellors talk of a contemplative listening to the people to whom they minister.[35]

When we approach prayer in this contemplative way, we are invited to focus solely on God and to let God do the work in us. Teresa of Avila says that, in contrast to other prayers where we have to work at drawing water from the well, this prayer is

---

34 Cited by James Gleick, *Isaac Newton* (London: Fourth Estate, 2003), 39. Newton wrote around 1670.
35 For example, William A. Barry, "The Contemplative Attitude in Spiritual Direction," *Review for Religious* 35, no. 6 (1976), 820-28. Gerald G. May, *The Dark Night of the Soul* (San Francisco, CA: HarperSanFrancisco, 2004), 127.

more like standing out in the rain, being soaked by the water.[36] However we pray such prayer, it seems God slowly frees us of ego, of the inner attachments described above (even without any awareness that this is happening) and leads us to a place of utter dependence on whatever God chooses to give us.

John of the Cross summarises contemplative prayer in this way:

> ... allow the soul to remain in rest and quietude... [We] must be content simply with a loving and peaceful attentiveness to God, and live without the concern, without the effort, and without the desire to taste or feel God.[37]

This was in John's treatise *Dark Night,* where he encourages desire for God, but distinguishes it from 'desire to feel God's presence'. For many, the temptation is to relieve the apparent dryness in the waiting time of the prayer by looking for some other way of prayer. In fact, John teaches that '(the dark night) is the secret way in which God not only liberates us from our attachments and idolatries, but also brings us to the realisation of our true nature. The night is the means by which we find our heart's desire, our freedom for love'.[38]

Such prayer seems to happen for us: we seem to be led into a more contemplative way of prayer. As well as the advice to 'pray as you are', Abbot John Chapman taught also to 'pray as you can – not as you can't'! We will know God's invitation to us

---
36 Teresa of Avila, "The Book of Her Life," in *The Collected Works of St. Teresa of Avila,* chapters 14 and 15.
37 John of the Cross, "Dark Night," in *The Collected Works of St. John of the Cross,* I,10.4.
38 May, *The Dark Night of the Soul,* 67.

by the prayer that seems possible for us. In my prayer, I tend to 'just sit' (as the Zen teachers say), to be present and focused. I don't claim any strong awareness of God, but on some level, I seem to know that it's good to be doing what I'm doing. Indeed, I find that I want to do it, I want to pray, I want God. Waiting on God and desire for God go hand in hand.

In the tradition of prayer, genuine desire for God is already to know God. For the desire is not at all possessive or wanting for oneself: it's more an openness, a readiness. And the knowing is not a knowing quite like we might have imagined, and certainly not a knowing in the usual way we come to know someone. Mahler captured this in his *Resurrection Symphony*: in the last movement, he has the soloist soaring above the chorus with the words 'what you have longed for is yours'.

Such prayer can seem quite empty in the praying. I remember John Chapman saying that the prayer time is so empty 'it feels like the completest waste of time'![39] It offers no great consolation in the sense of feeling delight or close to God. It is more likely to be painful because it is a time of dark emptiness, calling on deep faith. Constance Fitzgerald calls it the 'prayer of no experience', the prayer of silent waiting on God which, she says, 'radically changes a person and opens into new possibilities, new vision, a vast bottomless and incomprehensible future toward which hope reaches and love gives'. I once said that it felt more like God's absence than presence. To which my spiritual director replied 'only because you are imagining that God's presence has to be always warm

---

39 John Chapman, *Spiritual Letters* (London: Sheed & Ward, 1983), Appendix.

and comforting'! In fact, we are being invited to wait on God, even in quite dry, empty prayer times.

When Merton describes his prayer experience, cited in the previous chapter, he reminds us that 'the emptiness (in prayer) is only apparent':

> The absence of activity... is only apparent. Below the surface, the mind and will are drawn into the orbit of an activity that is deep and intense and supernatural, and which overflows into our whole being and brings forth incalculable fruits.[40]

The fruits that Merton promises, in fact, are God's gifts of growth in inner freedom and truth, emerging out of the apparent emptiness or darkness, in perfect parallel with the teaching of John of the Cross.

This prayer without images and without words is sometimes called 'the way of negation', negating or denying anything other than God, even the gifts of God. Even though there are numerous prayer practices (the prayer of the breath, the Jesus prayer, centring prayer) that might promote Merton's 'seeking the Face of the Invisible', it is not a prayer that we necessarily choose to pray, but rather one that we are called to or invited to by God.

The prayer practices referred to – centring prayer, the Jesus prayer – are designed to give a focus for prayer, usually in the form of a mantra. They aim to help us put aside or forget our human thinking and feeling and imagining. David Pennington's

---

40 Merton, *Seeds of Contemplation* (Wheathampstead, Hertfordshire: Anthony Clarke Books, 1961), 188.

work on *Centering Prayer*[41] stresses that in praying with a mantra, 'whenever in the course of prayer we become aware of anything else, we simply and gently return to the presence by use of the prayer word'. The prayer word or mantra, then, is a focus for our prayer to help us put aside all that is not God.

At the same time, I'm aware that many people find such prayer already happening for them (without their planning or choosing), as though they want to pray but just don't have the words, or feelings, or imagination. Clearly, they do have a desire for God. It seems that this desire, more than anything else, and even without any great consolation, is what sustains such prayer. This was the point made earlier in John of the Cross' treatment of the experience of Dark Night. Only our desire for God keeps us praying.

Spiritual directors know that the surest sign that the prayer is of-God (even without words or feelings) is its effect on the rest of a person's life. When we are led to pray contemplatively in this way, the prayer time may seem empty and without consolation, but it still bears fruit. As outlined above, people grow in love and acceptance of others, they become more compassionate, more practically caring, indeed more free. Then we can trust that relationship with God is healthy.

Karl Rahner has suggested that many of life's everyday experiences offer the same way to God. In his *Reflections on the Experience of Grace*,[42] Rahner talks of the experience of 'pure Spirit' – as distinct from the experience of Spirit as part of this

---

41 David Pennington, *Daily We touch Him* (New York: Doubleday Image Book, 1977) and *Centering Prayer* (New York: Doubleday Image Book, 1966).
42 Karl Rahner, "Reflections on the Experience of Grace," in *Theological Investigations* (New York: Seabury, 1967), 86-90.

temporal world, permeating or seasoning our earthly lives. And so, he calls it also an experience of the 'supernatural' or an experience of 'eternity'.

Some of Rahner's examples are useful:

> Have we ever kept quiet, even though we wanted to defend ourselves when we had been unfairly treated? Have we ever forgiven someone even though we got no thanks for it and our silent forgiveness was taken for granted? ... Have we ever been good to someone who did not show the slightest sign of gratitude or comprehension, and when we also were not rewarded by the feeling of having been 'selfless', 'decent', etc.?

In the earlier example, Walter would have to answer 'yes' to Rahner's last question. Rahner says such experiences are to taste the Spirit', to taste 'fullness in emptiness, life in death, the finding in renunciation'. But, clearly, we cannot predetermine such experiences; nor can we claim them as our own possession, as Rahner is quick to remind us:

> One can only look for it (this grace) by forgetting oneself; one can only find it by seeking God and by giving oneself to him in a love which forgets self, and without still returning to oneself.

This perfectly parallels Merton's 'seeking the face of the Invisible'.

Most importantly, the lesson is that it's all God's work, that God decides how we pray and how we relate. Most people find that they pray in both ways – the way of affirmation and the way of negation. Sometimes we find ourselves joyfully praising God in a liturgical celebration, then sitting in apparently empty quiet time; or we may find we are happy reflecting on some Scriptural text one day, but quite unable to pray in the same way the next. And for most of us, the experiences of pure Spirit that Rahner speaks of (the way of negation) are given to us only occasionally, and usually quite unexpectedly, as we go about the ordinariness of our daily living (the way of affirmation, affirming the gifts of God as a way to God).

This is the contemplative approach to prayer and to life. We don't have to work at being the people God calls us to be, so much as allow God to free us. Content with what is, counting our blessings and enjoying the gifts of life and love that surround us, surely prepares us for whatever else life has in store, whatever future choices life asks of us.

In what follows, I reflect on the same experience of apparent emptiness in our waiting on God's gift, interestingly, captured in a popular song.

The Sounds of Silence

> *'Go out and stand on the mountain before the Lord,*
> *for the Lord is about to pass by...'*
> *The Lord was not in the wind...*
> *the Lord was not in the earthquake...*
> *the Lord was not in the fire...*
> *after the fire, a sound of sheer silence.*
> *When Elijah heard it, he wrapped his face in his mantle,*
> *went out and stood at the entrance to the cave...*
> 1 Kings 19:11-12

The sound of sheer silence reminds me of the Zen koan about the sound of one hand clapping. I try to imagine what sheer silence would sound like – and I cannot get beyond words like emptiness, a void.

Ironically, thousands of words have been written in an attempt to describe silence! Maybe because there are no words? For the same reason, some have called upon the help of our other senses. For example, Simon and Garfunkel wrote their hit tune *The Sounds of Silence* in 1964. I remember only the opening line:

Hello, darkness, my old friend, I've come to talk with you again...

Silence is the absence of sound; darkness is the absence of light. Are they describing the same reality? The void?

In the void, God said, 'Let there be light' – and light emerged. For God, nothing is void (in our sense of the word): there is always something new emerging. There is light in darkness:

Even the darkness is not dark to you:
the night is as bright as the day,
for darkness is as light to you. (Psalm 139:12)

Light is revealed in darkness. In darkness, light emerges. In silence, music emerges.

In a very different area of study, eco-scientists add their support in their description of the Big Bang theory: 'there was emptiness – and it exploded!' Something new did indeed emerge.

There is no void for God. In God's way, new life is the constant promise: in every dying, there is the promise of life. I daresay this is why many have said that 'silence is the language of God'. God may well seem silent – and often does – but God's silence is God's way of communicating! We are invited to deeper faith, trusting that something is happening in us deep-down, something 'supernatural'.

It seemed sensible to check Simon and Garfunkel's lyrics. I was delighted to find these words. In a dream, they sang:

> *And in the naked light I saw*
> *Ten thousand people, maybe more*
> *People talking without speaking*
> *People hearing without listening*
> *People writing songs that voices never share*
> *No one dare*
> *Disturb the sound of silence.*

The song writer(s) offer unusual, but strong, images of sheer silence: 'people talking without speaking' and 'hearing without listening'. Their image is no easier to imagine than my image of the void, but I suspect that that is the point: sheer silence, God's silence, is not a human concept. It is not within human understanding or imagining. Again, we are being invited to a deeper level of communication, very different from our everyday experience, more 'communion' than what we usually think of as 'communication'. Simon and Garfunkel glimpse this deeper experience in the 'naked light', the light barely visible in the void.

John of the Cross had an image for that, too: the living flame: the flame of love that burns still, even in the darkness, and that purifies us and heals us:

> *Flame, living flame, compelling*
> *yet tender past all telling,*
> *reaching the secret centre of my soul!*
> *Since now, evasion's over,*
> *finish your work, my Lover,*
> *break the last thread, wound me and make me whole.*
>
> *Burn that is for my healing!*
> *Wound of delight past feeling!*
> *Ah, gentle hand whose touch is a caress,*
> *foretaste of heaven conveying*
> *and every debt repaying,*
> *killing, you give me life for death's distress.*
>
> *O lamps of fire, bright-burning*
> *with splendid brilliance, turning*
> *deep caverns of my soul to pools of light!*
> *Once shadowed, dim, unknowing,*

now their strange, new-found glowing
gives warmth and radiance for my Love's delight.

Ah! gentle and so loving
you wake within me, proving
that you are there in secret and alone,
your fragrant breathing stills me,
your grace, your glory fills me
so tenderly your love becomes my own.[43]

John is describing both the purification via the 'flame' and the freedom, the wholeness, the gift of God's tender love.

The naked light, the living flame, like the Easter candle, never dies. Alive and burning, the flame gives meaning to sheer silence, to the void of many people's experience. And to John of the Cross' experience. We are invited to trust that something new emerges, new life, free life. With Merton, we bow in silent adoration before this God who never fails us.

---

43 John of the Cross, *Centered on Love: The Poems of Saint John of the Cross*, 22-3.

The Contemplative Way

'Let the Spirit pray in you.' Gradually, we do become more able and more willing to let the Spirit pray in us, to let God take over... gradually we become more receptive, more open to God and to other people.

In the contemplative way, we wait on whatever will be revealed. We wait on God's inspiration. And we remain open to that revelation.

God slowly frees us of ego, of (our) inner attachments... and leads us to a place of utter dependence on whatever God chooses to give us.

The Way of Discernment

*Beloved, do not believe every spirit,
but test the spirits to see whether they are from God,
for many false prophets have gone out into the world.*
1 John 4:1-2

*If a white swan is given a mixture of milk and water to drink,
the swan will drink the milk and leave the water.*
Hindu saying.

Conflicting Spirits

In my early formation as a spiritual director, I was privileged to study with and be mentored by Jesuit priests William Barry and William Connolly who were prominent in the revival of the ministry of spiritual direction in the 1970s. In their classic work, *The Practice of Spiritual Direction,* Barry and Connolly define spiritual direction as:

> the help given by one Christian to another which enables that person to pay attention to God's personal communication to him/her, to respond to this personally communicating God, and to live out the consequences of the relationship.[44]

Living the consequences of our relationship with God asks an attentiveness to the ways that God is present to us and inviting us to ever new life. The presence of God's Spirit, permeating all life and all creation from the very beginning is the essential framework for my ministry:

> You spare all things, for they are yours, O Lord, you who love the living. For your immortal Spirit is in all things. (Wisdom 11:26 to 12:1)

> The Spirit is unique and present everywhere, transcendent and inside all things, subtle and sovereign, able to respect freedom and to inspire it. The Spirit can further God's plan...[45]

---

[44] William A. Barry and Willian J. Connolly, *The Practice of Spiritual Direction* (San Francisco, CA: Harper & Row, 1982), 8.
[45] Yves Congar, *I Believe in the Holy Spirit* (New York: Crossroad Publishing Company, 1997), II, 17.

To be fully present to all humanity and to all creation, to listen to the Spirit of God in all voices, invites quite significant inner conversion for many people. This can happen, for example, in ecumenical dialogue listening truly to voices quite different from one's own. Similarly, people experience the invitation to conversion in their relationship with the environment, the community of creation which they both care for and depend upon. All creation is sacred, made so in the very moment of creation, confirmed by Jesus shedding his blood over the earth and the ever-present Spirit of love holding creation as one. Such conversion is doubtless ongoing, as one is drawn into solidarity or oneness with all creatures.

This theology overcomes any hint of dualism and leads to a realisation of the sacredness of the earth and the full and equal humanity of women and men.

Awareness of God's presence and invitation deepens as we notice the inner movements in ourselves, the movements of the different spirits in our lives. Listening and noticing 'with the eyes of God', as we grow in inner freedom, we learn to sift through these movements – the felt needs and desires, the spontaneous impulses and affective habits, the thoughts, imaginings, emotions, attractions and repulsions in our experience of life – 'so that, through dealing properly with the experiences, one can find and be with God in every situation and moment of life'.[46] The sifting involves being sensitive to the movements, recognising and naming the movements, then understanding where they come from and where they lead. Then we are discerning.

---

[46] George Aschenbrenner, "Currents in Spirituality: The Past Decade," *Review for Religious* 39, no. 2 (1980): 198.

In the process of this sifting or separating, 'the fundamental principle is that the best guide is the discovery of the direction in which the interior movements lead'.[47] God's Spirit is alluring, always drawing towards God (Hosea 2:14). And so, the movements that come from the Spirit of God lead to wholesome life, to personal freedom, to loving relationships, ultimately to God:

> The fruit of the Spirit is love, joy, peace, patience, kindness, generosity, faithfulness, gentleness and self-control. (Galatians 5:22-23)

Further, the apostle Paul says that the Spirit of God is 'for building up the Body of Christ' (Ephesians 4:12).[48] God's Spirit is constructive, it builds. In other words, the gifts of the Spirit are given for the common good: because one moved by the Spirit of God becomes more loving, God's Spirit is seen to promote relationships, to build community (1 Corinthians 12:7 and 14:4, 12) and to work towards wholeness. Indeed, 'Love is a direct and privileged gift of the Spirit'.[49] I develop this experience of God's Spirit in the following chapters.

On the other hand, movements prompted by some spirit that is not-of-God lead to non-life, to isolation and loss of one's

---

47 Ernest E. Larkin, "What to Know About Discernment," *Review for Religious* 60, no. 2 (2001): 163.

Denis Edwards, *Breath of Life: A Theology of the Creator Spirit* (Maryknoll, NY: Orbis Books, 2004), 162. Denis Edwards, "Discernment of the Holy Spirit," *Presence* 13, no. 4 (2007): 21-29.

48 God's Spirit is said to be 'edifying', taken from the Latin word *aedificare*: to build.

49 Jacques Guillet, "Sacred Scripture in Discernment of Spirits," in *Discernment of Spirits* (Collegeville, MN: The Liturgical Press, 1970), 47.

inner freedom.⁵⁰ In the same Galatians text (5:22-23), Paul lists 'quarrels, dissensions, factions', the very opposite of the fruit of the good Spirit.

The challenge to us when sifting the movements of different spirits in our lives is that:

> ... these criteria are not exactly measurable. Each of them can be mistaken for other reactions... Mere relief at having made a decision can look like the peace of the Spirit, for example. Witless enthusiasm can look like joy. Apathy sometimes resembles patience. Peace can mean a quiet sense of inner freedom that results from openness to God and willingness to respond to God... but it can also mean no more than the absence of strong feeling.⁵¹

This necessary process of sifting or 'recognising and admitting differences'⁵² asks for a contemplative listening to the inner movements in one's self, both to recognise the movements and to come to understand their significance. Barbara Albrecht stresses that one's listening is not only with the ear. In listing the 'spiritual senses', she speaks of 'a nose for the things of God' needed 'to differentiate between good and evil, between true and false'.⁵³ Following St Benedict, Mary

---

50 I use the term 'spirits not-of-God' where other commentators refer to 'evil spirits', 'bad spirits', 'counter spirits'.
51 Barry and Connolly, *The Practice of Spiritual Direction*, 106, 109.
52 Ibid., 102.
53 Barbara Albrecht, "Discernment of Spirits," *Review for Religious* 38, no. 3 (1979): 388-89.

Margaret Funk calls this 'listening with the ear of the heart'.[54] David Stendl-Rast says simply 'a listening heart'.[55]

I discuss now how God's Spirit and spirits not-of-God work in human experience.

God's Spirit

Herbert Alphonso[56] focuses on one's 'personal vocation' as an expression of one's experience of God's call. I find this a useful framework in which to study the very personal, individual ways in which God's Spirit works in us. We discover these personal ways of the Spirit by reflection on the graced moments of our lives, the experiences of gift, the images that energise and call us to life, and the times of decision-making that have proven unquestionably life-giving. Reflecting on personal experience in these ways helps us to notice not only the fruits of God's Spirit working in us – the peace, joy, harmony that Paul describes (Galatians 5:22-23) – but also the signs in us when the Spirit is active and inviting – maybe the inner 'tingle' or excitement, the unquestionable 'knowing', the new level of energy, or the call to life.

I cited Walter's experience in an earlier chapter to illustrate growth in inner freedom. Looking back on that experience, the first sign that God's Spirit was inviting Walter was the sudden inspiration that he could live differently, without always being thanked for his generosity. His acting on that inspiration bore

---

54 Mary Margaret Funk, *Discernment Matters* (Collegeville, MN: Liturgical Press, 2013), 3, 71. Timothy Fry, ed. *The Rule of Saint Benedict* (Collegeville, MN: Liturgical Press, 1981), Prologue, verse 1.
55 David Stendl-Rast, *A Listening Heart* (New York: Crossroad, 1999), 1-7.
56 Herbert Alphonso, *The Personal Vocation* (Rome: Centrum Ignatianum Spiritualitatis, 1990).

good fruit, his 'lightness' and his different, freer relationship with his friend Wes.

Most often, people seem to recognise the fruits of the Spirit before they realise that they have, in fact, responded to the invitation of God's Spirit. Spiritual directors are well prepared to help people name these fruits, to deepen their awareness and appreciation of the felt 'good' or the 'peace', or sometimes the disturbing sense of being invited to new truth in themselves. These are experiences of *consolation*. In this terminology, 'consolation' is a technical word to describe an inner movement towards God, towards life – a movement, in fact, that is not always 'consoling', not necessarily 'peaceful'. Consolation may well come with painful challenge or with sad tears of some past mistake. What defines consolation is that it is always a movement towards God, always life-giving.

This movement towards God, towards wholesome living, will show itself invariably in the way the fruits of the Spirit overflow into our relationships. When we are true to the invitation of God's Spirit in our life, relationships flourish: we become more open to others, more accepting, more tolerant of others. As noted above, God's gifts are given to us personally, but not privately; the gifts are given personally, but for the sake of others.

Once the fruits have been recognised, it becomes possible to look back to name how and when God's invitation or God's gift was offered to us. Knowing that God's Spirit is quite consistent and faithful, it seems important to articulate the initial signs, not only for the sake of learning, but more importantly so that the same signs will be recognised in future experience.

Spirits not-of-God

And yet, we sometimes misread the signs; sometimes, unwittingly, we are deceived by other spirits, spirits that are not-of-God and that lead us away from life, more into confusion, isolation from others and lack of love. These are experiences of *desolation*, a technical term to describe a movement away from God. This movement away from God can happen despite ourselves: it is not a question of morality or a choice to sin.

We have discovered from experience how such a movement happens. For most of us, most of the time, spirits not-of-God aim at our vulnerabilities and our lack of inner freedom. A helpful Ignatian insight is that the tempter consistently targets our vulnerable spots: his image is the army commander attacking the weakest point of the enemy's fortress. Invariably, the temptation seems to come via false messages that we give ourselves: though the messages are quite false, they are heard as true, because they appeal to our vulnerability. This insight, confirmed in experience, has helped many people to understand how some of their life decisions have gone wrong.

To refer again to Walter's experience, his vulnerable spot was his attachment to his need to be thanked and affirmed. The inner messages Walter was hearing were 'he (Wes) doesn't appreciate me – he mustn't get away with that', 'I should be acknowledged and thanked'. Because of the inner attachment, these messages sound credible, though they are false.

As with the workings of God's Spirit, similarly with the spirits that are not-of-God, people often notice the fruits of the spirit first. It can happen, for example, that sincere decisions later turn sour – the 'fruits' turn out more destructive than life-giving. When we notice this, again it pays to look back to the time the decision was made and name the voice we were listening to in ourselves when we made that decision. Clearly naming that initial message will bring awareness also of the appeal the message was making. At least in retrospect, it is possible to recognise the point of vulnerability and why the message seemed true at the time. This is not to be self-critical or self-blaming: indeed, it seems important to acknowledge that the initial decision was made in all sincerity.

Only now, in retrospect, we are able to say that what seemed true, in fact, is false. Clear thinking is needed here: because the temptation came via false messages that we give ourselves, only true reasoning will counter the work of these spirits not-of-God. Only now, we can say clearly 'we do not, in fact, believe that message'. This is to sift the varying spirits in our experience, wanting to see truly, 'with the eyes of God' – for the sake of a wholesome life style.

Our vulnerable spots are quite personal: examples might be a need for affirmation, a sensitivity to criticism, a fear of what others think of us, a rigidity in relationships, a tendency to devalue oneself, all points of *unfreedom* or attachment, as described above. More often than not, our vulnerability connects with our self-esteem. And in some sense, this vulnerable spot or 'weak spot' in our make-up will always be with us, explaining the predictability about the way spirits not-of-God tempt with their false messages. When Paul begged God to take away his vulnerability – the 'thorn in his flesh' – God's word to Paul and to us is that it is better to leave it there, for then we are more likely to know the need for God's grace (2 Corinthians 12:7-9).

Even though we remain vulnerable, with growth in freedom and growing awareness of our vulnerability, our attachments do seem to lose their power. We become more free to make fruitful choices.

Spirits in Communal Experience

God's Spirit and spirits not-of-God work also in group experience.

A basic given is that every person has a contribution to make and a right to speak:

> ... each of us has an inner divine light that gives us the guidance we need, but is often obscured by sundry forms of inner and outer interference.[57]

> The whole body of the faithful who have received an anointing which comes from the holy one (cf 1 John 2:20, 27) cannot be mistaken in belief...[58]

My experience working with groups, however, has convinced me that a group is more than the summation of many individuals: the whole is greater than the sum of the parts. For

---

57 Parker Palmer, "The Clearness Committee: A Way of Discernment " *Weavings* 9, no. 4 (1988): 38. Palmer, prominent writer in the Quaker tradition, is cited in Wilkie Au and Noreen Cannon Au, *The Discerning Heart: Exploring the Christian Path* (New York: Paulist Press, 2006), 126.
58 Vatican II, "Lumen Gentium (Dogmatic Constitution on the Church)," in *The Documents of Vatican II*, #12.

there is a *group* experience of God's Spirit and of spirits not-of-God, a *group* identity, and a *group* vulnerability, over and above the individual experiences of the members of the group. I believe that any group wishing to discern God's call to them *as a group* must first establish and reinforce their 'common base', their communal identity.[59]

When facilitating groups, I spend considerable time building this foundation in the group, creating a listening community, even before the introduction of any question or decision that the group wishes to face. Essential to this step is the need to look at the interplay of relationships within the group and the influence of these relationships on the way the group, as a whole, approaches God.

Quality time given to prayer and listening in the group, discovering the workings of God's Spirit and other spirits not-of-God *in the group*, is foundational in this process. Facilitators ask only these pre-requisites: that all be willing to give time to prayerful listening, and that, to the best of their awareness, all come freely and open to God's Word.

***

In summary, noticing and interpreting the movements of different spirits in our inner experience rests on the habit of contemplative reflection. We grow in awareness of how we are 'moved' in our inner life and we learn from experience to interpret the movements – some lead to life (consolation), some to non-life (desolation). We are more able then to make

---

59 Brian Gallagher, *Communal Wisdom* (Bayswater, Vic: Coventry Press, 2018), 12, 43.

choices in the future. God's Spirit promotes life and truth, and challenges any falsity; while spirits not-of-God not only tempt us where we are unfree, but encourage *unfreedom* and untruth.

We experience the call to freedom and the fruit of being freed principally in our relationships with God and with God's people. A contemplative way of living, growth in inner freedom (via experiences of 'purification') and discernment are all *relational*. Contemplation is the desire to see and relate to others truly – indeed, to see 'with the eyes of God'. In turn, this desire invites us to relate from a freer place in ourselves. In this very desire to relate truly, we are 'purified' or freed. And, with the new awareness of where and how God calls us to inner freedom – and where we can be unfree and vulnerable – we become more discerning, more able to sift the spirits within us.

God's Spirit in the People of God

An experience in Melbourne some years ago helped me to clarify a key indicator of God's Spirit at work. In 2004, several institutions in Melbourne were celebrating 150 years. *The Age* newspaper celebrated its 150 years; the State Library was 150 years old; Victorian Railways turned 150 (the first steam train in Australia travelled the whole 10 kms from Flinders Street to Sandridge, Port Melbourne, in 1854); the old paddock called the Melbourne Cricket Ground was first levelled and mowed 150 years ago that same year; and Melbourne City Mission also was 150 years old that year.

Clearly, 1854 was a year of considerable energy and fecundity in Melbourne. But, I wonder, could all of these new beginnings be connected in any way? Is it coincidence or is it some kind of providence that would inspire such creativity in one small village called Melbourne?

It seems to me that the common thread through the newly founded Melbourne *Age*, the State Library, Victorian Railways, the MCG, and the welfare work of City Mission, is that they are all about giving people new hope, new life. They are all concerned with restoring dignity to God's people. At a time when the whole world was reeling from the mixed fruits of the Industrial Revolution, the populations in the cities were snowballing, many who used to be contented workers of the land had become the new poor, and the Gold Rush was in full swing in the tent-towns of Victoria, people needed hope.

I believe that, even in what initially appear as quite secular examples – travel, sport, culture, even care of the needy – the common threads that emerge in these apparently independent activities are sure indication of the Spirit of God at work. Much the same sign – people's yearning for hope and meaning, for recognition and belonging with other people – seems to pop up independently and, to all appearances, at random in all of these different places. Jesus called it *the signs of the times.*

If more evidence is needed of the ground-swell inspired by God's Spirit in 1854, there's yet one more sesquicentenary not to be overlooked: Eureka Stockade also celebrated 150 years. That uprising of the miners in Ballarat, led by Peter Lalor, in some sense stands as the Australian symbol of everyman's, everywoman's, right to justice and to fair treatment and to equality with every other man and woman. Again, it seems to me, it's about the human yearning for recognition and belonging. It's about restoring dignity to God's people.

That all people are equally loved by God – that all people belong in the one family of God – is not only our belief; it is our tradition. As in 1854, still today, people yearn for recognition and equality – instance the struggles of oppressed people in our world, the seemingly endless battle that the women of our world have even for equal pay for equal work, and the people who come to our spirituality centres praying for healing and for meaning in their lives. This clearly is the work of God's Spirit.

A passage from the book of Micah captures well what was going on in Melbourne in 1854: act justly, love tenderly, and walk humbly with God (Micah 6:8). Justice, love, and truth are God's prerogatives. We are blessed to be invited to share them – in the very different culture of today – as much as 150 years ago.

When the young man approached the old guru, asking to be a disciple, the old man said to him, 'Show me your wounds'. 'Oh', he said, 'I don't have any wounds'. 'What?', said the old man, 'has there been nothing worth fighting for?' Images of fighting and carrying wounds may not appeal to everyone, but there is no doubting the message that acting justly, loving tenderly, and walking humbly with God, costs. In some sense, we can expect wounds. Though the text says 'This is *all* that is asked of us', it isn't as easy as it sounds.

What is the cost? I believe the cost is the ongoing commitment that is asked of us if we are to live justly, love tenderly and walk humbly with God. Precisely because the fullness of justice, tenderness and humility belong in God, we grow into justice, tenderness and humility. It takes time. The fruit of this work of the Spirit of God in 1854 is evident in our lives now.

I have no doubt that in another 150 years, God's Spirit will be no less active: God's people will still yearn for recognition, for acceptance, and for oneness with all other people. God's Spirit will still inspire the invitation to act justly, love tenderly, and live humbly.

God's Spirit in Creation

God's Spirit works, too, in creation. It is strange paradox that we who are created beings can know something of the creator God, who is entirely 'other' than creation. Maybe unexpectedly, we experience the 'otherness' of God by living in and appreciating the tangible concreteness of our humanity and of all creation. It's a hard lesson to learn that only by living our humanity fully – not trying to put it aside – that we find God. And I suspect that when we are gifted with an experience of God's 'otherness', beyond our humanity, only then will we truly know our wholeness, our oneness, our unity with all creation.

I daresay we have all had glimpses of this. Whether crossing the Nullarbor or flying over Arnhem Land, I find myself totally absorbed in the sheer vastness and apparent emptiness of our country. It's as though I'm swallowed up by the land: I become one with the land, with God's creation. I seem to lose awareness of my self, my humanity. Similarly, I recall the time when I viewed in a museum an artefact that had been dated 16 centuries BC: in my astonishment, it was as if all time had merged for that fleeting moment — only that moment existed. And a very different example: I remember my first visit to a ward of terminally-ill old men in a psychiatric hospital where I was part-time chaplain. Though I was young and healthy, my immediate experience was that I belonged with those men: everything in me wanted to sit down on the floor where they were sitting, to be one with them, not remote from them, looking down on them. Now I see that in all of these experiences I'm drawn *into* my humanity, into creation and at the same time, *beyond* my humanity. Living my humanity fully and honestly is to transcend my humanity, to know God as other than human.

This is precisely the way of Jesus. Sebastian Moore understands that celebrated text in Philippians (2:6-11) about Jesus 'emptying himself' to refer to Jesus emptying himself of all ego, and so living his humanity fully. Moore paraphrases Paul's text:

> Jesus, being in the form of God (as all humans are)
> did not translate this into being for himself (as all
>   humans do).
> On the contrary, he took on our humanness in an
>   extraordinary way,
> its true way, a way of total self-dispossession, of
>   freedom from ego,
> in which (upsetting all our ideas of what befits divinity)
> he made manifest the ultimate mystery
> that itself is poor, for-all, has no possessions, makes
>   rank meaningless...
> which fact became fully manifest in Jesus raised from
>   the dead
> and receiving the name beyond all names.[60]

Living his humanity fully and truly, ultimately in death, Jesus was raised to life, God's life. And so, Paul sees Jesus crucified and raised to life as the true wisdom of God. (1 Corinthians 1:24, 30)

***

---

60 Sebastian Moore, *Jesus, the Liberator of Desire* (New York: Crossroad, 1989), 42.

One of the gifts of recent years has been a renewed and deepened awareness of the environment in which I live. Because of the location of my home and its environment, I seem to be more open to the changing seasons, the recurring patterns and indicators of approaching weather, the movement of the tides, and the beauty of my surrounds. I contemplate the sea daily, I'm entertained by the playful bird and animal life outside the window of my quiet space, I eagerly anticipate the cycle of blossoms and colours in my garden, and I lament the too-often storm damage as large eucalypt branches break and fall to earth.

I am but one member of this earthly community. Until his death last year, my long-time canine companion, Scobie, was another. Scobie and I always tried to care for the community to which we belong – indeed, we know it depends on us. Though, I fear, we can also threaten it: I think, for example, of Scobie's dislike of seagulls on the beach and the echidna who visits our backyard. And then I realise that the community cares for us, too – in some sense, we depend on it. And we, too, can feel threatened – by the strong north wind on high-risk bushfire days and by the otherwise-beautiful fox who kills our chickens. There is something about the mutuality and inter-relatedness of the community that seems to invite me more deeply into the heart of creation. If only fleetingly, I seem to touch our shared life, our communion. Dare I call this shared life God's life?

I believe I have sensed something of the same life of God in creation in those wonderfully gifted times when I visited the Kruger National Park in South Africa, the pre-historic stone monuments in Tonga, the pristine-pure Gordon and Franklin rivers in western Tasmania, and the temples of Kyoto in Southern Japan that seemed way beyond any human design or making. The echidna in my backyard, no less.

Such experience has been called the 'unspeakable closeness of God':

> If, in Jesus, God is revealed in specific human historical shape, in the Holy Spirit, God is given to us in a personal presence that exceeds the human and transcends human limitations. In the lovely phrase used by Moltmann, the Spirit is the 'unspeakable closeness of God'. We can experience this unspeakable closeness in moments of deep connection with a place, in times of delight in birds and animals... and when we stand in silence before the mystery of the universe... The Spirit is living water, untamed wind, blazing fire... and sees to the 'depths of God'. (1 Corinthians 2:10)[61]

Over many years, I have been drawn to a verse in Colossians (1:20):

> *Through him, God was pleased to reconcile to himself*
> *all things, whether on earth or in heaven,*
> *by making peace through the blood of his cross.*

The different translation that I grew up with refers to all things, all creation, *coming together*. I find confirmation of my experience in the theology of Karl Rahner and Denis Edwards. Following early Franciscan theology, they believe that God

---

61 Denis Edwards. *Breath of Life: A Theology of the Creator Spirit* (Maryknoll, NY: Orbis Books, 2004), 128.

chooses *from the beginning* to create a world in which the Word would be made flesh and the Spirit poured out. The incarnation does not come about as some remedy for sin, as in some other theologies, but incarnation and the gift of the Spirit are both central to God's purpose in creating:

> Creation, incarnation, and final fulfilment are united in one act of divine self-giving. This one act has specific and diverse effects and outcomes in the created order. It is a Trinitarian act of self-bestowal: God gives God's self in the Word and the Spirit, in diverse ways, in creation, grace, incarnation, and final fulfilment.[62]

Rahner and Edwards call God's self-giving, in love, *God's self-bestowal* – in creation, in incarnation and redemption, and in final transformation when all things 'come together'. This seems to me to be the foundation of our conviction that all creation is one – and is sacred. Made so, from the very beginning, by God's very act of creation, by Jesus shedding his blood, poured into our earth, and by the Spirit that finally transforms and reconciles all. God's life is, indeed, in all creation.

The Bible's Book of Wisdom sees God's presence in 'the structure of the world and the activity of the elements... the alternation of the solstices and the changes of the seasons, the cycles of the year and the constellations of the stars... the varieties of plants and the virtues of roots' (Wisdom 7:17-20). I believe in that presence: indeed, my belief that God's Spirit is present in all life, all creation, all human experience, is the

---
62 Denis Edwards. *Creation, Redemption, and Special Divine Action* (Hindmarsh, SA: ATF Theology, 2010), 39-42.

ground on which I build my habit of contemplation in order to be present and open to this Spirit of God.

***

Understanding the ways of God's Spirit and spirits not-of-God in our human experience, and learning to sift these spirits through growth in inner freedom, are basic steps towards living a discerning way of life. I discuss that now.

The Way of Discernment

God's Spirit is always alluring, always drawing towards God... (Hosea 2:14) And so the movements that come from the Spirit of God lead to wholesome life, to personal freedom, to loving relationships, ultimately to God.

On the other hand, movements prompted by some spirit that is not-of-God lead to non-life, to isolation and loss of one's inner freedom.

For most of us, most of the time, spirits not-of-God aim at our vulnerabilities and our lack of inner freedom... Invariably, the temptation comes via false messages that we give ourselves; though the messages are false, they are heard as true, because they appeal to our vulnerability.

The necessary process of sifting... asks for a contemplative listening to the inner movement in one's self, both to recognise the movements and to come to understand their significance.

A Way of Life

Integration is wholeness... It is healing.
It is self-possession, consolation, openness, freedom, detachment,
indifference,
a trusting spirit, and all the other fruits of the good Spirit.
The integration we speak of is the work of grace.[63]

Ernest Larkin

---

[63] Ernest Larkin, *Silent Presence* (Denville, NJ: Dimension Books, 1981), 46, 60.

Living 'in the Spirit'

For most of us, our senses tell us what we judge to be reality – we see and we touch, we taste and we smell... and we consider that what our senses tell us, in fact, *is* reality. But there is a reality, too, beyond our senses. For example, the times when we say that we 'sense' something happening or we sense someone's presence even in a pitch-black room when it is too dark to see (or touch, taste or smell). In other words, we 'sense' in a whole different way, maybe a deeper, truer way. Another example is the experience of knowing something we consider beyond any question, though we cannot prove it or convince anyone else. I call these experiences 'living in the Spirit'. In Andrew Lloyd Webber's song *The Music of the Night*, he calls it 'a strange new world', a life 'you've never lived before'.

In this new life, living in the Spirit, all we have are our 'spiritual senses': we listen 'with the ear of the heart', in St Benedict's phrase, or we see 'with the eyes of God'. Best of all, we have a 'nose for the things of God'.

I believe John of the Cross is speaking of the same experience in his poem *After an Ecstasy*:

> *I went into an unknown land*
> *unknowing, stayed there knowing naught,*
> *beyond the power of human thought.*
>
> *I know not where I entered in*
> *But when I found that I was there,*
> *not knowing how, not knowing where,*

> *strange things I heard, so deep within,*
> *far greater than I could declare.*
> *So there I stayed still knowing naught,*
> *far, far beyond all human thought.*[64]

This is indeed a 'strange new world'. I suspect that few of us call it 'ecstasy', but it is to live 'in the spirit', to live as we've 'never lived before'. In an earlier quotation, Thomas Merton describes someone who lives in the Spirit as one 'who is famished for truth and seeks to live in generous simplicity'. My reflection suggests that we are drawn into this newness, as we grow in freedom through our contemplative practice.

---

64 John of the Cross, *Centered on Love: The Poems of Saint John of the Cross*, 27.

A Discerning Way of Life

Growth in inner freedom bears fruit in our deeper self-awareness and easy familiarity with the ways of God's Spirit and spirits not-of-God in ourselves. We live a discerning way of life when this awareness is so integrated that honest loving response to God's invitation in our everyday becomes second nature. We then live the fruits of the Spirit (Galatians 5:25): we become more loving, kind, patient, by nature. We have grown in inner freedom.

John of the Cross does not have any formal teaching on discernment, though his principles are clear in a response he wrote to a community of sisters who had asked his advice about one of their members who was claiming special religious experience. John wrote of the 'five defects which he considers reveal that hers is not a good spirit':

> First, it seems that she has within her spirit a great attachment to possessing things... Second, she is too secure in her spirit and has little fear of being inwardly mistaken... Third, it seems she has the desire to persuade others that her experiences are good... Fourth, the effects of humility do not appear in her attitude... Fifth, the style and language she uses doesn't seem to come from the spirit she claims...[65]

In contrast, the indicators of a life lived 'in the spirit' that John of the Cross expects are detachment, openness,

---
65 John of the Cross, "Censure and Opinion," in *The Collected Works of St. John of the Cross*, 683-4. This is thought to have been written in the year 1588.

unpretentiousness, humility and simplicity. John is speaking of the inner freedom that comes from the Spirit of God, highlighted in his classic work, *The Dark Night*, described above.

Persons who live in a discerning way are free people, people free to love. Such people are in tune with the Spirit, they 'respond to what is good and true connaturally, congruently, by second nature. They resonate with what is of God, because they are of God.'[66] Their freedom or detachment shows itself in the way they relate to other people, to their ministry and to the struggles and joys of life. They appear to be more human, more deeply joyful and balanced, more likely to engender trust...[67]

With such people in mind, Ernest Larkin writes:

> Integration... is self-possession, consolation, openness, freedom, detachment, indifference, a trusting spirit, and all the other fruits of the good Spirit.[68]

Just as growth in inner freedom is gift of God's grace, fruit of attentive waiting on God, so too is one's sensitivity to sift the spirits, as discussed in earlier chapters. A key word in the description of such a person is 'integration'. Those who live in the spirit have integrated learnings and growth in freedom to the point where their relationships and responses to another are spontaneous and free. The gift they have received is described in this way:

> Discernment is defined as 'the process by which we examine, in the light of faith and in the

---

66 Larkin, *Silent Presence*, 29-30.
67 Barry and Connolly, *The Practice of Spiritual Direction*, 123-4.
68 Larkin, *Silent Presence*, 46, 60.

connaturality of love, the nature of the spiritual states we experience in ourselves and in others.[69]

I emphasise that the process of becoming integrated in this way and living a way of life in touch with God's Spirit is a gift of God's grace. Cooperation with grace asks a commitment to growing in awareness of our *unfreedoms* or inner attachments and to changing our habitual behaviour flowing from the places of *unfreedom*. It is in this context of living our freedom that John of the Cross urged 'denial' of our 'inordinate appetites',[70] and Ignatius Loyola encouraged acting against (*agere contra*) our 'inordinate attachments'.[71] In the earlier example from Walter's experience, Walter did just that: he acted against his inner attachment to be well thought of and acknowledged. Andre Louf argues that this is the proper understanding of 'fasting' in the Christian tradition: fasting from one's addiction.[72] Only gradually, as we build new habits of behaviour, discernment become connatural.

Fidelity to the contemplative way, openness to God, and deep desire to become free make possible such a way of life. As mentioned initially, only then are we able to make good decisions in life. I describe Christian decision making, sometimes called discerning God's will, in what follows.

---

69 Edward Malatesta, "Introduction to Discernment of Spirits," in *Discernment of Spirits*, 9.
70 John of the Cross, "The Ascent of Mount Carmel," in *The Collected Works of St John of the Cross*, 19.2 and 11.1. Iain Matthew, *The Impact of God*, chapter 7.
71 Ignatius Loyola, *Spiritual Exercises*, ##16 and 157.
72 Andre Louf, *Teach Us to Pray* (London: Darton, Longman & Todd, 1974), 82-6.

Making Good Decisions

I believe that the ways suggested for good decision making are of little value without the preliminary work of noticing and becoming familiar with the ways of God's Spirit and spirits not-of-God in one's whole life, as discussed in earlier chapters. For this reason, I believe that a 'living relationship with God', a contemplative openness to the Spirit of God, is the essential foundation for fruitful decision making and wholesome living.

Christian decision making or discernment of God's will is a collaborative process, built on relationship with God. It is not mere discovery of God's will. Edward Vacek develops the collaborative process within the context of a 'mutual love relationship with God':

> When Christians live out this relationship, the religious question is not primarily *what does God want?* or *what is good for me?* but rather *what should we (God and I) do?* or *what is appropriate to our mutual love relationship?* While God is the ontological originator, sustainer and inspirer of this relationship, we also have a contribution to make to its development and fulfilment.[73]

A commitment to knowing and carrying out God's desire does not exempt us from the human activity of listening to, growing awareness of, and interpreting the movements of the spirits in our inner experience. In any situation, God may

---

73 Edward Vacek, "Discernment within Mutual Love Relationship with God," *Theological Studies* 74, no. 3 (2013), 699.

well prefer one or other of the alternatives we face, but God's preference, God's will, is discovered only through the human work of growing awareness and growing freedom, described above and applied below. As Toner observes, 'Divine influence supplies us with what no human efforts could possibly achieve, but it does not replace those efforts'.[74]

In much of the writing, the treatment of decision making is more on the level of practical helps, rather than the actual step of making one's decision. For example, Mark Thibodeaux lists 'typical phases' involved in any process of discernment: get quiet, gather data, dream the dreams ('tapping into deep desires'), ponder the dreams ('weighing consolations and desolations').[75]

Mary Margaret Funk offers 'five steps to making a decision' from the monastic tradition:[76]

> We ask the Holy Spirit to help, even to clarify the question we are facing.
> We make a virtual decision, a tentative answer that seems the most likely solution.
> We ask for a confirming sign, as we 'live into' the decision.
> We then make our decision, taking action, even ritualising the decision.
> And finally, we watch thoughts and guard our heart, especially guarding against second thoughts of doubt or recalculating risks.

---

74 Jules J. Toner, *Discerning God's Will* (St Louis, MO: Institute of Jesuit Sources, 1991), 38.
75 Mark Thibodeaux, *God's Voice Within* (Chicago. IL: Loyola Press, 2010), 152-76.
76 Mary Margaret Funk, *Discernment Matters* (Collegeville, MN: Liturgical Press, 2013), 3, 71.

Francis de Sales stresses the basic pre-requisites in Christian decision making. Francis outlined 'a short method to know God's will' in his *Treatise on the Love of God*. He insists that we must wait on God's revelation, be open to whatever God asks, and be prepared to follow God's good pleasure without question. Francis sees the temptation to doubt one's decision as the work of some spirit not-of-God.[77]

Accepting these helps to decision making, I now focus on the actual moment of making one's decision. As an example, this is Syd's experience:[78]

> **Syd**, *a young committed scientist, unmarried, was head-hunted and offered a new position in marine biology research, the area of his interest and expertise. The position was in a branch of CSIRO, fully government funded, recently established in Antarctica. Syd sat with the offer for a couple of days and decided that he would accept – even before he had talked with anyone else about this offer of a new job. Syd said, 'It just felt right'.*
>
> *Questions came when Syd did begin to tell people. Syd's parents reacted quickly. They reckoned he was crazy: why move to a place called Sorin ('never heard of it!') in that freezing climate? 'It couldn't possibly be good for your health.' Syd's present boss could not understand why Syd would accept such a pay cut. And Syd's cricket mates felt let down: Syd is easily their best batsman and he must know the struggle the team is having even to stay in the competition.*

---

77 Francis de Sales, *Treatise on the Love of God* (Rockford, IL: Tan Books, 1963), chapter 14.
78 This fictitious example was used initially in *Set me Free*, 2019, 207-9.

> *Syd came to talk with me, recommended by a mutual friend. He began by saying that he thought he had made a good decision till 'all these objections came up'.*

One way of decision making, often encouraged, is to compare the advantages and disadvantages of the options that one faces. Syd could do that easily. This new job offer seems to have more disadvantages than advantages. Indeed, staying in his present position appears to have the advantages – no disruption, a steady salary and certain future, a good social life and good friends. Were Syd to follow this method of making his decision, he may well decide to reject the offer of the new position.

Another way of making decisions is more affective than rational. This way works on the level of inner reactions. Syd had said that 'it just felt right'. Our conversation continued:

> *'Syd, what are you actually feeling when you say that your decision felt right?' Syd struggled to name his feeling. Words came slowly: 'It felt right... like good and true... maybe I felt at home with the possibility, at ease, comfortable... even contented. It's hard to put words on feelings, isn't it?' 'OK', I said 'so what you are saying is that feeling comfortable and content with the thought of the new job seemed right to you. I wonder what makes it right? Is it a familiar feeling for you? You must have felt this before?' Syd said, 'I don't think I have put words on it quite like I have now, but yes, I do know this feeling. Even in little decisions every day, whenever I feel like this, I know I'm in the right place.' I could see that Syd was trusting his own past*

> experience, fairly spontaneously recognising that this inner experience, however difficult to articulate, was actually a sign for him of the right way to go. Because it had paid off in the past. This seemed more important to Syd (and to me) than all the arguments for and against such a decision.
> I asked Syd about the different reactions of his friends. He reckoned that he could understand what they were saying and he would certainly want to be sensitive in his helping them to accept his decision. But 'I believe that if this is best for me, it will end up being good for others, too.' 'OK, so where are you now?' I asked. Syd said quickly, 'Oh, I'm going. I'm excited about the new possibilities. I'm looking forward to contributing to some worthwhile research.'

In Syd's experience, the two ways of making his decision, the more rational and the more affective, would appear to result in different outcomes. Syd has learned from past experience to 'trust his gut', even though he finds it difficult to explain. It is very personal: the signs of what is right for Syd are unique to Syd.

Interestingly, the traditional treatment of ways of decision making in Ignatius Loyola's *Spiritual Exercises* includes both of the possible approaches that Syd faced. Ignatius offered three ways or 'times' for making a 'good choice' in life.[79] Ignatius places his teaching on decision making after a succession of meditations that he recommends to ensure that one comes to

---

79 Ignatius Loyola, *Spiritual Exercises*, ##175-8.

the decision making exercise quite freely.[80] I discuss Ignatius' three ways of making a decision in what follows.

Ignatius' first way

In the **first way** suggested by Ignatius, discovered in his own experience,[81] God 'so moves and attracts' one's will that the decision to be made cannot be doubted. Ignatius gives Paul's conversion experience on the way to Damascus and Matthew's responding to Jesus' call as examples of this way of making a decision. Roger Haight suggests that Ignatius' examples are rather too 'supernaturalistic', risking one's overlooking 'ordinary human decisions'.[82] More everyday examples might be a person's clear, unmistakable decision based on some unexpected gift of God in prayer or in a dream, when one 'knows' God's invitation with certainty. My experience affirms that people do sometimes know, without any doubt, the decision they need to make in a particular situation.

In fact, in this way of decision making, the decision makes itself. The second and third ways of making a decision outlined below are quite different: they rest upon a person's familiarity with the ways of the spirits in one's life and the principles discussed above.

---

80 These are the meditations on 'Two Standards' (*Spiritual Exercises*, ##136-148), 'Three Classes of Men' (##149-157), and 'Three Kinds of Humility' (##165-168)
81 Toner, *Discerning God's Will*, 109-10. Toner reflects on Ignatius Loyola's experience recounted in his *Autobiography*, #27
82 Haight, *Christian Spirituality*, 224.

Ignatius' second way

Ignatius' **second way** is based on affectivity, when a decision is made 'through experience of desolations and consolations and discernment of diverse spirits'.[83] This is the most common way for making decisions. In practical terms, this way involves noticing and listening to the movements of affectivity in one's inner life when prayerfully considering the alternatives one is facing, as in Syd's example above.

I have learned from experience that the alternatives one is facing in a decision to be made need to be considered *one at a time*, and sometimes over fairly prolonged periods. One needs to sink deeply into each alternative, to live it as though it were the decision already made, and to notice the movements associated with that alternative. All one's previous experience of consolation and desolation, then, becomes the reference point for interpreting movements associated with living the alternatives of this decision to be made: which alternative 'fits' with what one already knows of the ways of God's Spirit in one's experience and which alternative 'jars'?

Rahner has Ignatius express the process in this way:

> When I placed the available possibilities and their potential outcomes before me in light of the impending free choice to be made, I discovered that one option clearly fitted into the wide freedom of God and remained transparent toward him, while the other did not, even though all options could be small signs of this infinite God which, each in its own way, derived from him. While it is

---

83 Ignatius Loyola, *Spiritual Exercises*, #176.

difficult to make clear, this is approximately how I learned to distinguish... between what held the incomprehensibility of the infinite God who wanted to be near me and what remained somewhat dark and non-transparent toward God...[84]

We remain 'transparent toward God' by noticing our experience of consolations and desolations in relation to the alternatives before us. We sift the spirits in this way, as outlined in my image of the white swan separating the milk and the water.

Syd's experience was an example of how personal, even unique, a person's affective reactions to the alternatives faced can be. Others will say 'it's not rational'!

This way is quite different from the third way, which is more rational. Interestingly, many people find that the third way, noticing the advantages of the two alternatives, will often confirm a decision made in the second way.

Ignatius' third way

The **third way** of making decisions is needed when a decision has not been made in either the first or the second way. Ignatius says this way is called upon only in a 'time of tranquillity', meaning that there are no affective reactions to the alternatives under consideration. A decision cannot be reached in the second way and so one has to turn to one's 'natural powers'.[85] Still presuming an attitude of openness, and still after honest prayer, one decides which is the 'more

---

84 Karl Rahner, *Ignatius of Loyola Speaks*, translated by Annemarie S. Kidder (South Bend, IN: St Augustine's Press, 2013), 19.
85 Ignatius Loyola, *Spiritual Exercises*, #177.

reasonable' alternative by weighing the pros and cons, the advantages and disadvantages, of the alternatives.

Though many people consider this way of making decisions to be less favoured than the second way, some say 'of limited usefulness',[86] at best, a 'last resort',[87] some others do still prefer this way. In my experience, this third way is unsatisfactory when used alone. Invariably, both alternatives under consideration will have advantages and disadvantages. When does one have enough advantages? How many more advantages than disadvantages are needed to make a decision? I am supported in this by Rahner who believes that 'reliance on pure reason is a deficient mode of discerning'.[88]

In summary, good decision making can happen in one or other of three inter-related ways:

First way	A time when God's gift cannot be doubted	The decision 'makes itself'
Second way	A time when one finds affective movements in oneself in relation to the alternatives	Decision is made by noting the inner movements in oneself, the consolations and desolations, when contemplating the alternatives

---

86 Larkin, *Silent Presence*, 31, 34.
87 Stefan Kiechle, *The Art of Discernment* (Notre Dame, IN: Ave Maria Press, 2005), 41. Valles, *The Art of Choosing*, 86. Edwards, *Human Experience of God*, 109.
88 Karl Rahner, *The Dynamic Element in the Church* (New York: Herder & Herder, 1964), 103, 08. See also Vacek, "Discernment within Mutual Love Relationship with God", 692.

| Third way | A time of 'tranquillity' when there are no emotional reactions to the alternatives | Decision is made rationally, listing pros and cons of the alternatives and weighing against one another |

Whichever way is used, however we negotiate our life's choices, openness to the invitation to the Spirit of God rests on growth in inner freedom in order to sift the spirits, as discussed in earlier chapters. As our inner freedom and our ability to discern the spirits become more integrated in our everyday living, decision making flows spontaneously. We then live a discerning way of life.

A Way of Life

In this new life, living in the Spirit, all we have are our 'spiritual senses': we listen 'with the ear of the heart', in St Benedict' phrase, we see 'with the eyes of God'... we have 'a nose for the things of God'.

Growth in inner freedom bears fruit in deeper self-awareness and easy familiarity with the ways of God's Spirit and spirits not-of-God in ourselves. We live a discerning way of life when this awareness is so integrated that honest, loving response to God's invitation in our everyday becomes second nature.

A key word in the description of such a (discerning) person is 'integration'. Those who live in the Spirit have integrated learnings and growth in freedom to the point where their relationship and responses to another are spontaneous and free.

The ways suggested for good decision making are of little value without the preliminary work of becoming familiar with the ways of God's Spirit and spirits not-of-God in one's whole life.

Conclusion

A way of life that is ever attentive to the different attractions and drives in our inner life – the different spirits at work – rests on growth in inner freedom. Though we are essentially free people, the human experience is one of limited freedom. The places of *unfreedom* in our make-up, explained in terms of our unconscious attachments or inner needs, make us vulnerable. Such vulnerability is ripe ground for any attractions in us that are not in our best interests, not life-giving. Growth in inner freedom is vital to healthy wholesome living.

Such growth in inner freedom comes through fidelity to a contemplative way of living and praying, openness to God, and deep desire to become free. As we grow in freedom, we are awakened to knowing beyond doubt that God is with us and that the *ruah* or Spirit of God permeates and unites all God's creation. With this growth and this awareness, we become more sensitive to God's Spirit in our lives, indeed more able to read the unique personal signs of the Spirit's invitation. Gradually, discernment of spirits and an ability to make life-giving decisions become second nature.

The Holy Spirit is already in us and in our world. God's life and love is already in us and in our world. The gift of awakening is that we are drawn into this mysterious love that permeates all creation and unites us as one:

> From the heart of Jesus, pierced on Calvary, I see a new world coming forth – a great and life-giving world inspired by love and mercy, a world which the Church must perpetuate on the whole earth.[89]

---

[89] From the meditations of Jules Chevalier MSC, around the time of his beginning the religious congregation, the Missionaries of the Sacred Heart, 1854.

Afterword

My first publication was entitled *Floatability Studies of Calcium Minerals*. It was the outcome of my two years research towards a Masters degree in Science in 1961. My mentors at the time were encouraging me to continue research work in chemistry and metallurgy towards a doctoral degree. I knew in my heart that that was not where I belonged. Instead I joined the religious congregation called the Missionaries of the Sacred Heart and began a further seven years of study towards priesthood.

After my ordination, my superiors couldn't resist: I was sent to teach science to teenagers. Within a year, they too knew that that wasn't where I belonged. Instead, I began a ministry of accompanying others in more personal ways, counselling young people, directing retreats, guiding men preparing for religious commitment. I then had the opportunity for excellent formation as a spiritual director. What some have called my life's work had begun.

In a sense, I did become a teacher – not in science, but in the life of the Spirit. Eventually, I did do doctoral studies – not in metallurgy, but in discernment of spirits and spiritual direction. This latter has been the focus of my ministry and my writing for fifty years. I don't consider myself a writer, but it seems I keep writing. When I ask myself 'why?', the only motivation I can think of is that I want others to know the good news that I have heard. Indeed, I can say, with St Paul, 'an obligation is laid on me, and woe betide me if I do not proclaim the Gospel' (1 Corinthians 9:16).

Over the years, I have learned and been supported by countless companions on the journey, friends, teachers, supervisors, my own spiritual directors, my students and those who have entrusted their experience to me in spiritual direction. I am ever grateful. My writing is the fruit of the learning of those years. As I have insisted, if this is the work of God's Spirit, it is meant to be shared. I am more than happy to pass it on now.

I acknowledge also those who have encouraged, advised and supported me in my writing. I thank especially Peter Price of happy memory, Patricia Fox and Alan Niven, Sue Richardson and Mary Coloe, Jill Manton, Annemarie Reiner and Frank Andersen, all trusted colleagues. Thank you also to Maree and Tom Leyden, meticulous proof readers. The journey continues.

Brian Gallagher msc

Appendix

Awareness Examen

The Awareness Examen prayer is a time of contemplative prayer focusing not on what I judge I have done well this day, but on what *God* has done in my life today. In practical terms, the prayer is best prayed at the end of each day, for maybe ten to fifteen minutes. It will involve:

- An expression of gratitude for the day and an openness and willingness to be led by God's Spirit right now

- A time of quiet relaxing and slowing down of body and mind, helped by slower and deeper breathing

- Then a conscious prayer, asking the Spirit to bring into my awareness whatever of the day – an event, a person, something that happened to me, a mood, a new insight – that God wants me to listen to again

- Having asked, I wait (*most people simply allow the experience of the day to flow back into awareness, quite freely, sometimes asking questions of God – where were you most active in my life today? how have you been moving in my heart today? have you been calling me or challenging me in special ways today? Note that I do not review the day myself or make my own judgments about the day; I wait on God.)*

- God has ways of bringing to my attention whatever God wants me to listen to: sometimes via a memory, or a person who comes into my awareness, or some feeling that I notice in myself. I gradually become more sensitive to noticing God's ways in my life

- Whatever comes to me, I simply let myself stay with that: I re-live it, savour it, maybe more than I did during the day, I allow it to touch my heart, all the time asking for God's message to me, God's revelation to me right now

- At some point, quite spontaneously, I respond directly to what I have heard from God: maybe a prayer of gratitude, maybe sorrow for some lost opportunity, maybe a prayer of trusting surrender, or a plea for help. I trust whatever prayer comes

- Most people then like to conclude with a verbal prayer of gratitude or praise of God, perhaps the Our Father

Acknowledgments

The chapters on *Freedom in Human Experience, A Discerning Way of Life* and *Making Good Decisions* are adapted from my book *Set me Free: Spiritual Direction and Discernment of Spirits*, 2018.

The chapter on *Contemplation* includes extracts from an earlier work *Taking God to Heart*, 2008.

Sections on *The Ways of the Spirits* and *Communal Discernment* are adapted from *Communal Wisdom*, first edition, 2009, revised and expanded, 2018.

The Appendix, *Awareness Examen*, is taken from my book *Pray as you are*, 1999.

Recommended Reading

John of the Cross

Dark Night in *The Collected Works of St John of the Cross*, edited by Kieran Kavanaugh and Otilio Rodriguez (Washington, DC: Institute of Carmelite Studies, 1973).

Centred on Love: The Poems of St John of the Cross, translated by Marjorie Flower OCD, (Varroville, NSW: the Carmelite Nuns: 1983, reprinted 2002).

> See also: Iain Matthew, *The Impact of God* (London: Hodder & Stoughton, 1995).
>
> Gerald May, *The Dark Night of the Soul* (San Francisco: HarperSF, 2004).

Thomas Merton

Contemplative Prayer (New York: Herder & Herder, 1969).

Spiritual Direction and Meditation (Collegeville, MN: Liturgical Press, 1960).

> See also: Brian Gallagher, "Thomas Merton: the Reluctant Mystic" in *Mystics for Every Millennium* (Heart of Life, 2002).

Brian Gallagher

Pray as You are   Collins Dove, Burwood Vic, 1990.

   Nelen Yubu, Kensington NSW, 1999.

   Heart of Life, Box Hill, Vic, 2012.

Taking God to Heart St. Pauls Publications, Strathfield, 2008.

   Heart of Life, Box Hill, Vic, 2013.

Communal Wisdom (second edition)

   Coventry Press, Bayswater, Vic. 2018.

Set me Free: Spiritual Direction and Discernment of Spirits

   Coventry Press, Bayswater, Vic. 2019.

www.ingramcontent.com/pod-product-compliance
Lightning Source LLC
Chambersburg PA
CBHW051955290426
44110CB00015B/2246